A TREE FOR TROUBLES

Cheryl Johnson

Illustrated by Katarzyna Surman

OneEarth Publishing

A Tree for Troubles

978-0-9911554-4-6 (Paperback)
978-0-9911554-5-3 (eBook)

Illustrations by Katarzyna Surman

Publishing Services, AuthorImprints.com

This is a work of fiction. The events and persons are imagined. Any resemblance to actual events, or to persons, live or dead, is purely coincidental.

Published by OneEarth Publishing, San Diego, California
http://www.theoneearthproject.com

This book is dedicated to trees, givers of life.

There once was a man with many troubles.

Every day, after a long day of work, the man would arrive home carrying his troubles with him.

One day, after work, instead of going straight home, the man decided to stop at a tree he loved, a tree that stood tall and strong on the hill above the town square...a tree that he helped plant as a child.

He wasn't sure what made him stop, but once he got to the tree, his troubles seemed to pour out of him, while the sturdy tree seemed to lovingly absorb them. That night, for the first time in as long as he could remember, he carried no troubles home with him...even if it was, just for the night.

So, the man found himself talking to the tree almost daily, and after doing so, he felt much better.

One day, a little girl saw the man talking to the tree and asked him what he was doing.

The man shared that he told the tree his troubles, and it made him feel much better. The little girl asked if she could tell the tree her troubles, too. The man thought that would be fine.

Now you might not think that a little girl would have many troubles, but you would be mistaken. Being a little girl can be hard, especially if you are worried about doing well in school, making and keeping friends, your parents arguing, and scary things that go bump in the night. So, the little girl found herself talking to the tree almost daily, and after doing so, she felt much better.

One day, an old woman saw the little girl talking to the tree and asked her what she was doing.

The little girl shared that she told the tree her troubles, and it made her feel much better. The old woman asked if she could talk to the tree, too. The little girl thought that would be fine.

Like little girls, you might not think that an old woman would have many troubles, but you would be mistaken. Being an old woman can be hard, especially if you are alone too much, don't feel well, or worry that you are no longer needed. So, the old woman found herself talking to the tree almost daily, and after doing so, she felt much better.

One day, a teenage boy saw the old woman talking to the tree and asked what she was doing.

The old woman shared that she told the tree her troubles, and it made her feel much better. The teenage boy asked if he could talk to the tree, too. The old woman thought that would be fine.

Like the young girl, and the old woman, you might not think that a teenage boy would have many troubles, but you would be mistaken. Being a teenage boy can be hard, especially if you are worried about being good at things boys are supposed to be good at, insecure about how you look, and afraid that you do not fit in. So, the teenage boy found himself talking to the tree almost daily, and after doing so, he felt much better.

Soon word spread, and everyone wanted a chance to talk to the "Tree for Troubles." So much so, that long lines of people formed, as people from far and wide began to converge on the small town for their chance to talk to the tall, strong tree...and be free of their troubles.

Sadly, there were so many people that the man, the little girl, the old woman, and the teenage boy could no longer even get near the tree.

Then one day, on his way home from work, the man noticed it. The tall, strong tree no longer looked tall or strong. Instead, it looked weary and burdened from the enormous weight of its branches; branches that were struggling to hold all of their leaves—more leaves than he had ever seen...on any tree. There were thousands of leaves where there had been hundreds, and it was obvious to the man that the tree would soon not be able to hold even just one more.

When the man went home that night he felt extremely troubled. He could see that the tree could not carry the burden of its enormous amount of leaves much longer. And, he could not help but conclude that the amount of leaves had to do with the people's sharing of their troubles.

Could it be, he thought, that the tree held the people's troubles in its leaves, and that there was a leaf for every trouble?

Believing this must be the case, and believing he was the one who had started the trouble, the man got dressed, and went out into the night to visit the tree.

As the man approached the tree, he was overcome with immense joy, and worry. He was filled with joy because he was reunited with his friend, the tree, and worry because of the tree's desperate, burdened state. As he was talking to the tree and confessing how sorry he was for being the cause of the tree's trouble, he was startled to see another person slowly approaching. It was the old woman.

The old woman slowly made her way up the path to the tree. The man, who had never met the old woman before, was surprised to see her, surprised to see anyone, out that late at night. Once she was at the tree they immediately understood why both of them had come— their shared worry for the tree.

The two began to talk and began sharing all that had been troubling them, including their worry over the tree. And, it was then that they noticed it, as they shared their troubles with each other instead of the tree, leaves began to fall from the tree. The more they shared, the more the tree shed its excess leaves...the more it shed its burden.

It was at that moment they knew what needed to be done to save the tree.

The next day, the old woman and the man told as many people as they could to meet under the "Tree for Troubles." This time not to share their troubles with the tree, but instead to share with each other.

Hundreds of people responded and gathered under the tree. Once assembled, they began to share with old friends and new. The more they shared, the more of the tree's excess leaves were shed, until the tree was completely free of its burden, their burden it had been lovingly carrying for them. The leaves dropped from the tree until it once again looked like the old tree the man had always loved.

To this day, people gather under the "Tree for Troubles," no longer to share their troubles with the tree, but instead to find a friend, sometimes a new one, with whom to talk and share. Sometimes people share their troubles and sometimes they share their triumphs, but everyone is happier because they have a place, and people, with whom to connect, and with whom to share.

The End.

Why I Wrote This Book

I wrote *A Tree For Troubles* for a couple of personal and heartfelt reasons—I wanted people to know they were not alone with their troubles, and I wanted people to see how healing it can be to seek out support in their community.

It is my hope that this story will inspire you to gather in your own community, like the people did in the story, to connect and support one another. Find a tree (or your version of a tree) in your neighborhood, at your spiritual center, at school, in a city park, or any place that strikes you as fitting for a place of healing and community. Make it a refuge, a gathering place that people, young and old, seek out if they need to find someone with whom to connect and share.

We are not alone. We are never alone.

Get Connected

- Join our A Tree for Troubles group on Facebook!
  https://www.facebook.com/atreefortroubles/
- Follow us on Twitter! **https://twitter.com/treefortroubles**
- Follow us and contribute on Instagram! **@atreefortroubles**
- Visit our website **www.atreefortroubles.com**

Thank you, trees, kind givers of life, our wise teachers. Peace to you all.

www.ingramcontent.com/pod-product-compliance
Lightning Source LLC
Chambersburg PA
CBHW060842270326
41933CB00002B/174